The Cradle of the Real Life

~ WESLEYAN POETRY

The
Cradle
of the
Real
Life

Jean Valentine

WESLEYAN
UNIVERSITY PRESS
Published by
University Press of New England
Hanover and London

Wesleyan University Press

Published by University Press of New England, Hanover, NH 03755

© 2000 by Jean Valentine

Printed in the United States of America

5   4   3   2   1

CIP appear at the end of the book

Grateful acknowledgment is made to the following periodicals in which these po-
ems first appeared: *American Poetry Review, Boston Book Review, Controlled Burn,
Field, Global City Review, Hayden's Ferry Review, Kenyon Review, Massachusetts Re-
view, Painted Leaf Press, Provincetown Arts, Ruah, Salamander, Southern Review,*
and *Third Bed.* To the editors, and to the MacDowell Colony, Yaddo, and Dorland
Mountain, my deep thanks.

For Jane Cooper and Adrienne Rich

with affection old and true

❧   So long as the heaven of *Thou* is spread out over me the winds of causality cower at my heels, and the whirlpool of fate stays its course . . . No deception penetrates here; here is the cradle of the Real Life.

—*Martin Buber*

Contents

Part I

The Pen

The sandy road, the bright green two-inch lizard
little light on the road

the pen that writes by itself
the mist that blows by, through itself

the gourd I drink from in my sleep
that also drinks from me

—Who taught me to know instead of not to know?
And this pen   its thought

lying on the thought of the table
a bow lying across the strings

not moving
held

Elegy for Jane Kenyon (2)

Jane is big
with death, Don
sad and kind — Jane
though she's dying
is full of mind

We talk about the table
the little walnut one
how it's like
Emily Dickinson's

But Don says No
Dickinson's
was made of iron. No
said Jane
Of flesh.

Black Wolf

Suffocated in the country
a sheep in my own curtain
wolf curtain!

The black wolf nobody else saw I alone saw
trotting down the lane past our house
—Black Heart! Don't go past our house

don't get lost just when I've found you
just when life is not afraid
any more. Of me. Just when —

(I didn't *need* to hate them. You can't beat a stick.
But nobody else could see what they were like.

See it wasn't all
"on the green hill sheep
kneel and feed")—

Mother Bones

B. is dragging his mother's bones
up the stone stairs
in a bag of grass cuttings.
But you can't grow
grass from cuttings.

They lead me

They lead me to a
"lovely nurse"
"in case B. needs her"
she is   I am
sugary
melt
and disappear

I ask for a dream
about my marriage:
"Ink." Ink. Ink. Ink.

My ink-stained hand
his paint-smudged hand

gone   where
nothing joins

Your mouth "appeared to me"

Your mouth "appeared to me"
a Buddha's mouth
the size of a billboard

I thought: of course,
your mouth,
you *spoke* to me.

Then your blue finger,
of course it was your finger,
you painted with your finger

and you painted me with your finger . . .

Then appeared to me flames:
transparencements of every hand and mouth.

Mare and Newborn Foal

When you die
there are bales of hay
heaped high in space
mean while
with my tongue
I draw the black straw
out of you
mean while
with your tongue
you draw the black straw out of me.

Truth

Sharing bread
is sharing life
but truth—
you ought to go to bed at night
to hear the truth
strike
on the childhood clock
in your arms: the
cold house
a turned-over boat,
the walls
wet canvases . . .

October Premonition

October premonition

seeing my friend leave
I turn my head up, away

if she has to leave
let me not see her

my leaving mother
leaving my door open a crack
of light   crack of the depression world

Rodney Dying (3)

I vacuumed your bedroom
one gray sock
got sucked up   it was gone

sock you wore on your warm foot,
walked places in, turned,
walked back

took off your heavy shoes and socks
and swam

November

November
leaving Ireland

Sligo Bay and the two mountains
the female and the male
walking down the stairs
into the ground

—I have to leave
and I have to watch.

Labrador

Crossing a fenced-off railroad track
holes in the fence
carrying a dog
my journey
I drop him
he's heavy   I can't pick him up

he puts his foot in a trap
chained to the track   a trap
yes   but that dog
won't chew his foot off
he's barking at himself   he won't let
me near.
         I left him.

1945

A year in the Pacific
watching his pilots
not come back to the ship

—they were nineteen, twenty,
they called him "Pop" . . .

We lived
for the day he came back.
The day he came back

he raged like Achilles

the day   the year   years

we flew off

one off a bridge   one into a book
one a note
into a bottle

we never came back.

—Oh my dead father
—Ah Jeanie, you're still in words . . .

Leaving

The dark black line
around the darker brown
ball of your eye

—I could only look at one eye at a time
like a horse:
white ring around the eye:

terror.
Eight years I sat on my heels in the field

waiting for you.
I *wanted* to.

Running for a train

Running for a train
an older woman on my back
another old poor woman
needs help to make it too
but I can't help her too
the train has started already
the engineer
is a young woman   she
looks out the window implacably
and keeps on driving
                        I knew her
I knew the old poor woman
still back at the other end of the platform
the woman slipping from me   I knew
the moon-faced boy watching by the side of the tracks

The Welsh poet

The Welsh poet
said of his mother
who "left the world"
last week
"She was never dead
in or out of it."
He shows me a beautiful Indian bird
red with yellow dots on it:
Happiness. Beauty. Art.
—That bird seems to like you.
—Yes, that bird knows
there's not much time.
The mother has a gold body now.

Radio: Poetry Reading, NPR

I heard your voice on the radio
thirty years dead
and got across the kitchen to
get next to you
breath and breath
two horses

But it wasn't you back then
I was liquid to,
it was my life:
I wanted to *be* you.
Amount to something.   Be

the other
the ready stone
—prayer-rag tied to a wire fence, a branch . . .

The Tower Roof

No music
no memory
not all your art
not   not
your iron story
can fold you into the galaxy

saved by yourself
lost by yourself

your iron words
hero and chorus

This far and no farther.

For a Woman Dead at Thirty (2)

In memory
you
go through that
door and go through that
door and go through that
door

cold
dark

and then the way
the sky is lightest
over water

this world lightened

as your words
opened into their third
star-darkness

The Blind Stirring of Love

I rub my hands my cheeks
with oil   my breasts
I bathe my genitals, my feet
leaf and bark

redden my mouth to
draw down your mouth
and all along
you have been inside me
streaming
unforsakenness . . .

Little Map

The white pine

the deer coming closer

the ant
in my bowl
—where did she go
when I brushed her out?

The candle
—where does it go?

.

Our brush with each other
—two animal souls
without cave
image
or
word

The Drinker

You   breathless
drinking   drinking

making for the door
out of your life

heading out through the
chimney   the body-hole

out from the house   the skin and
bone   out from

the silence
—Love

won't take you out   death
won't take you out

nothing that's the same
will take you out

The Drinker (2)

In the doorway
your face a candle

Your face a white island
between the two currents, between the
falls of your black hair

You who drank your life greedily
hole never filled

Girl-woman who could not
whose lips could not open

Hungry ghost in the doorway

Your bones might as well have flown together and spoken:
Where is she whom my heart loves?

—Oh my darling,
where do you look for me?

Happiness

Remember our happiness?
under us   happiness
under the city
under our fathers' graves   happiness
under this world
under the gospel of the evangelist John :
This is the happiness he leaned his head against.

Happiness (2): The I Ching

(Alone)
"Unconcerned"
"Undaunted"

Sunset
sunrise
pines
hermit thrush

Central Park, Billie Holiday
—Misfortune. No blame

—the boat pond
rises
above the trees

: the dead don't go away
: you   "   "   "

He leaves them:

He leaves them:

No nothing's happening
you   why do you
get angry   cry
why are you leaving Me, he cries:

He turns into a moon
They turn into night bandages
He turns into strips of film
blue with another woman's blue
—loses the blue

Away from you

Away from you,
alone, I *can* come

—a leaf flickers
on the river's light skin

Together
we are two stones like one stone rolling

rolling down on the riverbed   two
light black stones

we have always been here
once we *were* one stone

—the other thing holds us
in its mouth

Child

You are in a blind
desert   child

your "too-muchness" is written
in the Torah

child   it is written
in the pit

written in black fire
on white fire

deer star
black star

third star
who sees

Part II   *Her Lost Book*

I.

Embryo

Still mermaid
inside   her
words only
half gathered

her head still floating
listening   listening
                    to the Real Life

The Women's Prison

The women in the prison
are combing mannequins' heads of hair
for Beauty Care.
It's cold in there
a prison necklace of noose and lies

This bodily tool of governments
the tooth pit   the grave

In the Public Library

In the Public Library
a woman is reading a factory story
several people listening
she gets to the fire
the noise   to the locked doors   the death room
The librarian says she has to stop
it's time for him to close. He closes.

Margaret, d. 1985

At the back of the church
dressed like a bag lady, Margaret
in dark torn clothes
with her old woman smell
with the red open wound on her forehead
maggots in her wound . . .

Third floor walkup on 112th
she may have been there 85 years
the steel door open to
cat shit cat food
human shit human food
ghost dust ghost Margaret

holding tight
to her iron bed
and to empty us
of every illusion of separateness,
on her forehead
the maggots' miner's lamp . . .

At the Conference on Women in the Academy

The young scholar, her weeping finger
the anger reality
under the "social construction of reality"
under the deaf blind TV filmed
broadcast auditorium: the woman talking
in the split-open room
under the room of what we say.

The Orphanage Landing

Goldenbridge, Dublin

We her countrypeople are deep asleep
we meet in the local
and talk in our bread-and-butter
sleep. All night the young girl waits
on the orphanage landing as Sister told her
till She comes   down the stairs
with a strap   with scalding water

In the morning the local doctor
covers the wounds up over and over
("called to the orphanage 71 times
in that year")
                        White wolves
run in: *No no this never happened.*
(White wolves in every second house are saying:
This is not happening.)

Reading the Mandelstams

Snow falling the sixth night
on the stone house full of silence
Why can't they drive you both now, tonight
up to the house, light up the house

Lines of ice
in the night window
notes

He Says to Me, In Ireland

He says to me, In Ireland
you've fallen into your destiny.
He says
the teaching and giving readings
night and day
keep him from the void. I say,
But you write about the void. I say,

All these women,
your mother,
two wives, a lover,
have died miserably,
and you have lived to write about it
your history of the world.
Or leave it out.

But I want those women's lives
rage   constraints
the poems they burned
in their chimney-throats
The History
of the World Without Words
more than your silver or your gold art.

What God Said

After she died
her son destroyed her paintings:
incinerator flames: "She wouldn't want anyone
to see this stuff." Then killed himself.

Do not fear your death, for when it arrives
I will draw my breath and your soul will come to me
like a needle to a magnet.

St. Mechtilde of Magdeburg

2.

Some of the signs suggest that you feel a leaf or
other part of a plant. A string leads from the top
of the sign to the plant.
—Braille sign on the Miwok Trail, Muir Woods

She wrote a book. Lost to us.
Her lost book said,
"Your search to find words
that will devour meaning
will devour you."
                    Her lost book said,
"I spent, and I earned, too:
But my money was no good there."

If my mother was one
and my sister was one
and my father
was not one
and my brother was not one
what was I?   I followed
the string in the dark. Alone:

Before the expected street into town
before the ramp Contentment
whose handrails budded long before birth
and grew ahead of me like arms
—I stopped like a horse.

Something bad is happening.
No one says anything.

One by one
they get up and walk away.

They promised not to know.

Generation to generation,
bone to bone.

Poetry

You, poem
the string I followed blind
to leaf by thick green leaf
to your stem
milky
poem without words
world electric with you

The Church

"Thank you for the food," we said,
it was mashed potatoes, gravy, this
was the place the regular people came,
to go through the regular
funnel. Leaving
I saw ———— and his red
candle of "find it." My life.

I couldn't
he couldn't

Father I'm twenty

Whiskey   marriage
children   whiskey

Alcohol alcohol alcohol
two children   hungry

depression's lead box
no air to breathe

Our therapist:
"You're married to a brilliant man,
you just have to accept it."

I was dark and silent.
The therapist said,
"Why don't you wear lipstick?"
To J: "Does she lie on top?"   To J:
"Don't *play her role.*
Don't give the children their baths
or feed them."

The soul has no   'other afternoon'
amiga gold
We   then
bandage her feet
as she steps   down and down
past where her parents pray for her
two still dark figures   kneeling in Gemini

Here there is no language

Drink   cut my wrists
drink take bad pills
into the locked ward   take good pills
can't feel   can't
or speak
or step

doctors looking down a well

The Locked Ward: O. T.

Poster paints, big brushes
like my girls' kindergarten brushes:
I make a big picture, primary colors:
the social workers come like kindergarten teachers
and ask me to explain it, I do, they say,
You don't need to be here.

—Where should I be?

On the mental floor
I painted a picture of the children
irreducible   altered
the MISSING children
but it was me missing.
Chewing up the mirror   the mother
was not someone else.

To the half-way house.
Protestant. I made
maple syrup. My friend moved in
with my husband and children.
The Methodist minister: How many men
do you have in your life.
—Sir   none.

Single Mother, 1966

No money
—the baby birds'
huge mouths
huger than themselves
—and God making
words
words

Abortion Child

I thought:
You live somewhere
deeper than the well
I live down in.
Deeper than anything from me or him.

No but it took me
time to see you, thirty earth years.

3.

To Ireland

By the Granary River
the landlord says,
"All these things —
the lambing — the commonage —
are good — yes — but they are not God."
Looking out over us
with a white and English eye.

Oh yes they are but
by the Granary River
we shut down seven hundred years.
My mother was in it, and hers, and hers,
my great-grandmother, hers died in the black room,
and her mother, mother to mother,
shut down and opened wrong.

Home

I left my clothes
and books
my skin
a snake
—the only one in the country!
Our sign
life   twice

Scarab rolling a ball of dung
across the ground
scarab hieroglyph:
to come into being:
scarab rolling with the sun
across the sky
Atlantic

No one's a house
for me anymore
or me for them
Home   not words but
I know it on my lips
it will come   it will melt
like ice on a stove   and I will drink it.

You walk across your self
as you walk across a dirt road
crossroads at dusk
and across a field   outsider
a field   and a field
steps go beside you   the sun
crossing a line   sun kind to you   sun you.

Under
water
look up at the dots of the sun run
along on the other side of the water line

under the white pine
the stars run along
on the other side of the sky's line   no lines

Snow
falling slow
filling our footprints

writing a word

changing it

night
at the window
two birches, blown together.

Snow falling
off the Atlantic

out towards strangeness

you
a breath on a coal

UNIVERSITY PRESS OF NEW ENGLAND

publishes books under its own imprint and is the publisher for Brandeis
University Press, Dartmouth College, Middlebury College Press, University of
New Hampshire, Tufts University, and Wesleyan University Press.

ABOUT THE AUTHOR

Jean Valentine won the Yale Younger Poets Award for her first book, *Dream
Barker*, in 1965. She is the author of eight books of poetry, including most recently
The River at Wolf (Alice James Books, 1992) and *Growing Darkness, Growing Light*
(Carnegie Mellon, 1997). She teaches at Sarah Lawrence College, the Graduate
Creative Writing Program at New York University , and the 92nd Street Y.

LIBRARY OF CONGRESS CATALOGING-IN-PUBLICATION DATA

Valentine, Jean.
The cradle of the real life / Jean Valentine.
p.   cm.— (Wesleyan poetry)
ISBN 0-8195-6405-2 (alk. paper) — ISBN 0-8195-6406-0 (pbk. : alk. paper)
I. Title. II. Series.

PS3572.A39C73 2000
811'.54—dc21   99-86176